Seeing Inside

Photographs

by

Joan Halifax

Axle Contemporary Press   Santa Fe, New Mexico

Published by Axle Contemporary
P.O. Box 22095
Santa Fe, New Mexico 87502
www.axlepress.com

© 2012 Joan Halifax, Upaya Zen Center/Institute
All rights reserved.

ISBN: 978-0-9858116-0-0

Edited by Jerry Wellman
Designed by Matthew Chase-Daniel and Jerry Wellman

Gratitude to Northwest Coast artist Joe David for inspiration to create this work.

At dusk, the sky washed with gold light

I was near sleep but awakened

To take in what will pass

Soon enough

When I was a kid, I got really sick. For two years, I couldn't see. It was then I discovered I had an inner world, and it was a visual one. Since I was born with two good eyes, I knew the visual experience. Then suddenly, one morning, I felt my way down the hall of our house in Coral Gables, Florida, my hand sliding along the wall, and told my parents that I couldn't see.

A cascade of physical disabilities followed and after a while disappeared. During the time when I was in bed, recovering from an unidentified virus, another world opened up to me. I began to re-create the outer world inside of me; I began to see inside.

When I got better, my mother and father gave me a Kodak Brownie Box Camera. Just as my interior life had appeared to me when I was sick, here was a little box that would capture what I saw. It could see inside. I was fascinated, and I was hooked. And I began to photograph the world that caught my eye, beginning from the age of six on, and now I am 70.

Today, a collection of nearly a hundred thousand photographs exists, a thread of images that span time and the world. When I was a kid, I photographed my handsome father standing proudly beside his Lincoln Continental. Soon thereafter, I photographed Cologne Cathedral with my Brownie. The haunting black and white image captured a heavy sky hanging ominously over the bombed cathedral. Recent photographs portray the faces of Tibetans, riven with the elements, Burmese elders, incandescent with innocence, and the landscapes of Zen and the Himalayas.

I never cared about or studied f/stops and shutter and film speeds. I only cared about composition and connection. I never took a class in photography, though I had friends who were great photographers, including Robert Frank, Ralph Gibson, Julio Mitchell, and others. I thought Diane Arbus was nothing but courage, and met her several times when I lived in New York. I was a huge fan. I loved the work of Ansel Adams and traveled with his daughter. Dorothea Lange's photographs always took my breath away, as did the work of Gordon Parks and Eugene Smith. In the 70's, I stayed in Eliot Porter's house on occasion in Tesuque, and studied his work. More recently, the photographs of Matthieu Ricard show a view of space and light that is resonant with my Buddhist practice. Yet, though the work of other photographers interested me, I had no interest in emulating anyone. I just did my own thing, privately and joyfully, capturing light, seeing inside

As I lived with the camera, the camera was not only my eyes but also my heart. It captured and held light, light that I was always seeking and finding, light that filled the world, even the world of suffering, when light shines through the darkness.

When I was in my twenties, I discovered meditation. What a surprise! It was not so different than the gift of my childhood blindness. I could, through meditation, see inside. I could also see the world in a different way, a way the camera had taught me. The camera had given me a view, a view that accepted everything into its lens. I had a viewfinder (meditation), and a way to develop the world or action. View, meditation, action are one way that Buddhism is described. It is a summary of the Eight-fold Path of the Buddha. And it was to become my way of life, and the life I have followed and noted through my friend, teacher, and constant companion, the camera.

Joan Halifax
June 13, 2012, Prajna Mountain Forest Refuge

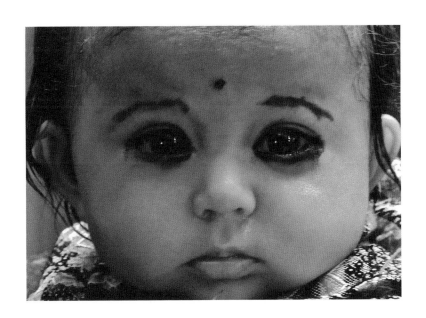

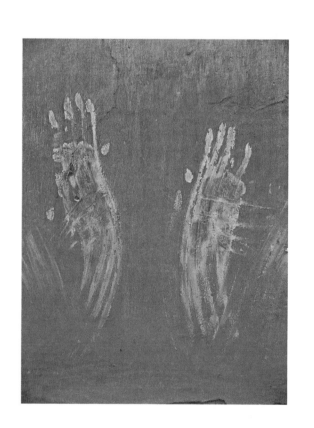

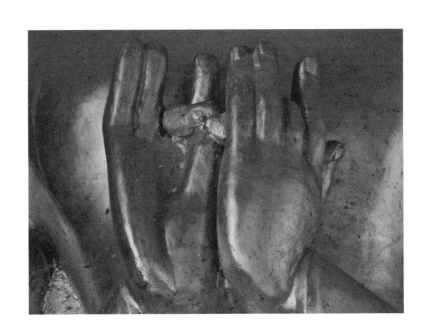

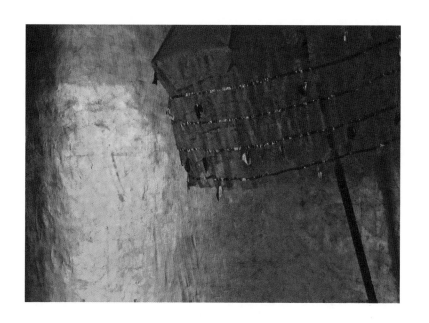

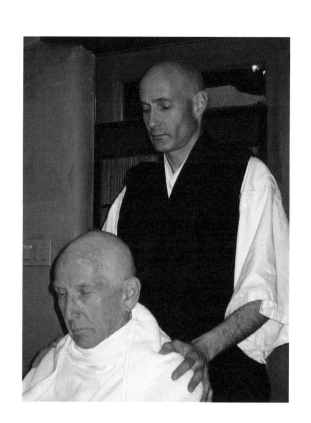

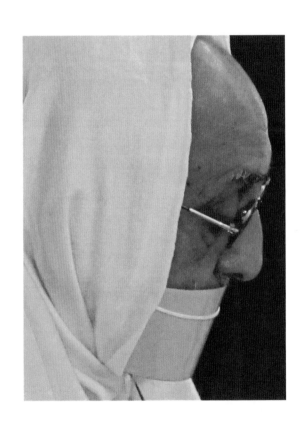

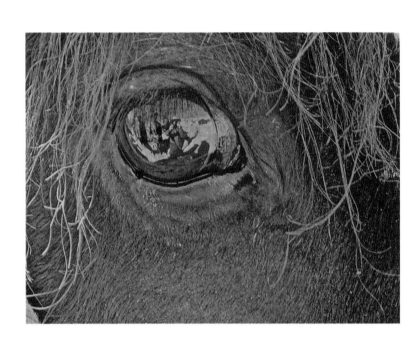

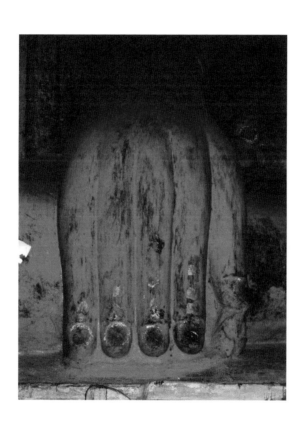

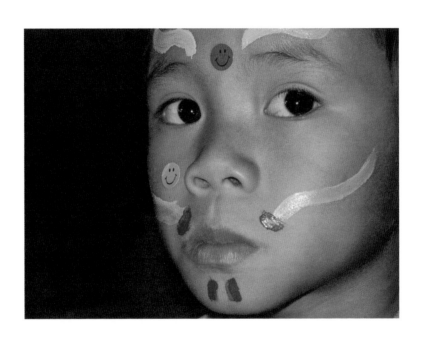

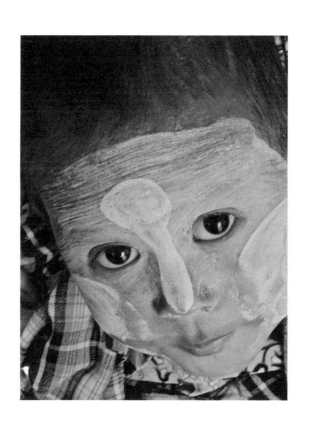